BASSOON

FILM FAVORITES

Solos and Band Arrangements
Correlated with Essential Elements® Band Method

Arranged by
MICHAEL SWEENEY, JOHN MOSS and PAUL LAVENDER

Welcome to ESSENTIAL ELEMENTS FILM FAVORITES! The arrangements in this versatile book can be used either in a full concert band setting or as solos for individual instruments. The SOLO pages appear at the beginning of the book, followed by the BAND ARRANGEMENT pages. The supplemental CD recording or PIANO ACCOMPANIMENT book may be used as an accompaniment for solo performance.

ISBN 978-0-634-08690-8

HAL•LEONARD®
CORPORATION

7777 W. BLUEMOUND RD. P.O. BOX 13819 MILWAUKEE, WI 53213

T0052580

00860142

PIRATES OF THE CARIBBEAN

(A medley including: The Medallion Calls • The Black Pearl)

BASSOON
Solo

Music by KLAUS BADELT
Arranged by MICHAEL SWEENEY

4

MY HEART WILL GO ON
(Love Theme From 'Titanic')

BASSOON
Solo

Music by JAMES HORNER
Lyric by WILL JENNINGS
Arranged by JOHN MOSS

00860142

THE RAINBOW CONNECTION

BASSOON
Solo

Words and Music by
PAUL WILLIAMS and KENNETH L. ASCHER
Arranged by PAUL LAVENDER

00860142

MAY IT BE

BASSOON
Solo

**Words and Music by EITHNE NI BHRAONAIN,
NICKY RYAN and ROMA RYAN**
Arranged by JOHN MOSS

From Walt Disney Pictures' TARZAN™

YOU'LL BE IN MY HEART

BASSOON
Solo

**Words and Music by
PHIL COLLINS**

Arranged by MICHAEL SWEENEY

00860142

From the Motion Picture SHREK 2

ACCI--ENTALLY IN L--VE

BASSOON
Solo

**Words and Music by
ADAM F. DURITZ**

Arranged by MICHAEL SWEENEY

Moderate Rock

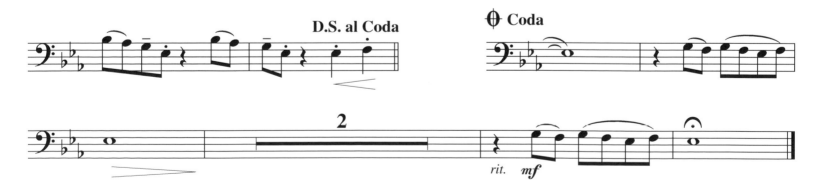

00860142

ALSO SPRACH ZARATHUSTRA

BASSOON
Solo

By RICHARD STRAUSS
Arranged by MICHAEL SWEENEY

Broadly

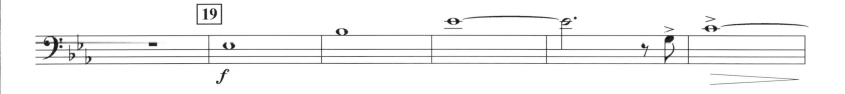

00860142

From the Paramount Motion Picture MISSION: IMPOSSIBLE

MISSION: IMPOSSIBLE THEME

BASSOON
Solo

By LALO SCHIFRIN
Arranged by MICHAEL SWEENEY

From SHREK
MUSIC FROM SHREK
(A medley including: Fairytale Opening • Ride The Dragon)

BASSOON
Solo

Music by JOHN POWELL
and HARRY GREGSON-WILLIAMS
Arranged by JOHN MOSS

"Fairytale Opening"

Gently

21 **With determination** "Ride The Dragon"

32

40

00860142

From the TriStar Motion Picture THE MASK OF ZORRO
Z-RRO'S T EME

BASSOON
Solo

Composed by
JAMES HORNER
Arranged by JOHN MOSS

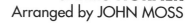

Heroically

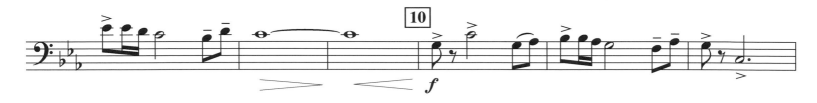

PIRATES OF THE CARIBBEAN

(A medley including: The Medallion Calls • The Black Pearl)

BASSOON
Band Arrangement

Music by KLAUS BADELT
Arranged by MICHAEL SWEENEY

00860142

14

From the Paramount and Twentieth Century Fox Motion Picture TITANIC

My Heart Will Go On

(Love Theme From 'Titanic')

Music by JAMES HORNER
Lyric by WILL JENNINGS
Arranged by JOHN MOSS

BASSOON
Band Arrangement

From THE MUPPET MOVIE

THE RAINBOW CONNECTION

Words and Music by
PAUL WILLIAMS and **KENNETH L. ASCHER**
Arranged by PAUL LAVENDER

BASSOON
Band Arrangement

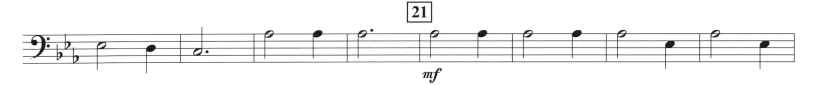

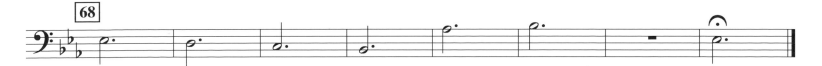

00860142

From THE LORD OF THE RINGS: THE FELLOWSHIP OF THE RING

MAY IT BE

BASSOON
Band Arrangement

Words and Music by EITHNE NI BHRAONAIN,
NICKY RYAN and ROMA RYAN
Arranged by JOHN MOSS

00860142

From Walt Disney Pictures' TARZAN™
YOU'LL BE IN MY HEART

BASSOON
Band Arrangement

Words and Music by
PHIL COLLINS
Arranged by MICHAEL SWEENEY

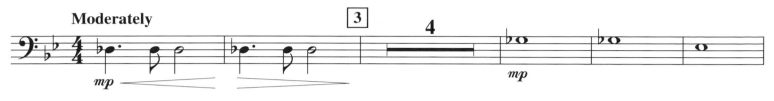

00860142

From the Motion Picture SHREK 2

ACCIDENTALLY IN LOVE

BASSOON
Band Arrangement

Words and Music by
ADAM F. DURITZ
Arranged by MICHAEL SWEENEY

Moderate Rock

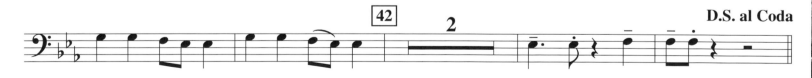

00860142

ALSO SPRACH ZARATUSTRA

By Richard Strauss
Arranged by MICHAEL SWEENEY

BASSOON
Band Arrangement

00860142

From the Paramount Motion Picture MISSION: IMPOSSIBLE

MISSION: IMPOSSIBLE THEME

BASSOON
Band Arrangement

By LALO SCHIFRIN
Arranged by MICHAEL SWEENEY

Moderately Fast
(3 + 2)

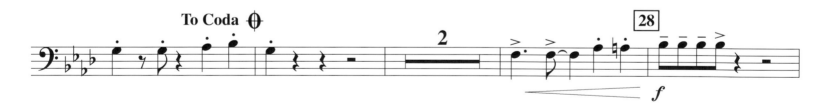

From SHREK
MUSIC FROM SHREK
(A medley including: Fairytale Opening • Ride The Dragon)

BASSOON
Band Arrangement

Music by JOHN POWELL and Harry GREGSON-WILLIAMS
Arranged by JOHN MOSS

00860142

From the TriStar Motion Picture THE MASK OF ZORRO

Zorro's Theme

BASSOON
Band Arrangement

Composed by JAMES HORNER
Arranged by JOHN MOSS

Heroically

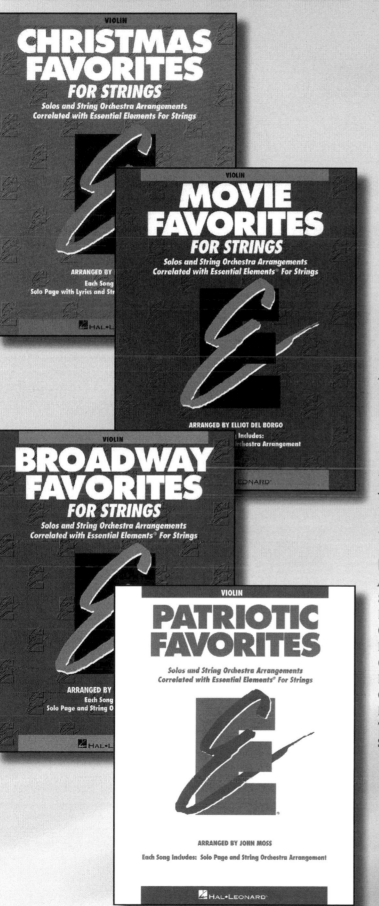